Creating Meaningful Wedding Design
A Bride's Guide To Wedding Decorating Like a Pro

Niki Thornton

Table of Contents

"Inspiration can come from anywhere. I've designed events getting inspiration from pieces of patterned paper, a favorite color, favorite painting, colored glass, animals. Anything can be inspiration. You will only be limited by your imagination."

- Niki Thornton

INTRODUCTION

This book is designed as a step-by-step guide to design for the do it yourself bride. From the chapters, you will learn how to come up with floral, table and room designs using items and colors you already love and surround yourself with regularly. It is not designed to give you specific design ideas but to give you a foundation on which to build. These methods can be adapted to any design style and any mood you want to create for your day. From this guide, you can decide if you want to do it yourself or hire a professional.

NOTE: Do not purchase/rent any items until you finish reading this book and doing the exercises. Good overall design comes from good planning.

Creating Meaningful Wedding Design
A Bride's Guide To Wedding Decorating Like a Pro

WHERE TO FIND INSPIRATION

EXERCISE

Go around the house and find five of your favorite
things. Take note of color, pattern, shape, texture,
scent, etc. This is your starting point. Take your items
and think of ways to incorporate them into your
wedding design or theme.

If you are unable to do the exercise, use the favorite
things list to come up with ideas. Create list for both
yourself and your fiancé. Remember it's his day too.

Photo: *Example of a favorite things list*
Colors, Artwork, Scarf, Jewelry, Gem, Scent, etc.

*As a result, a color scheme emerged in burgundy,
orange, gold and cream*

My List of Favorite Things

Favorite Color(s): _____
_____

Favorite Flower: _____
_____

Favorite Pet, Insect, reptile, etc.:
_____
_____

Favorite Scent(s): _____
_____

Favorite Plant: _____
_____

Favorite Shape: _____
_____

Favorite Artwork, Sculpture, Vase, Photo, etc.:
_____
_____

Favorite Texture: _____

Favorite Gem: _____

Any Other Elements You Love:
(Heck, Favorite Elements: Gold, Silver, Copper...):
_____
_____
_____

CHAPTER ONE

ROOM DESIGN

Step One: Book Your Venue(s) first!

You can't begin to design your wedding until you know where it will take place. The principles in this book can work for wedding inside and outside.

> **NOTE:** In selecting your venue, you don't want to book a venue too large for the invited number of guest. Choosing a venue too large will make your room feel empty and less inviting and will cost more to decorate. Also, keep in mind that your setting should be intimate without feeling crowded.

Step Two: Take photos and measurements of your room(s) to refer back to later. Taking photos will assist you at times when you can't remember every detail about your room. Measurements will assist you in coming up with your floor plan.

Step Three: Take note of the architecture of your venue(s). You will need to address elements you would like to hide in your design, as well as elements you would like to emphasize.

For a venue with columns, consider up-lighting using bulbs in your favorite colors. If there are items on the walls that can't be removed, consider wall panels or drapings to hide them. Incorporate items from you favorites list, like putting some artwork on the walls in coordinating colors. A less expensive alternative, that I have used in many designs, is patterned paper in frames. Scarves with designs could also be an option. Mirrors on the wall create a sense of depth and reflects light(ing) back into your space.

NOTE: In your design, try to keep your main colors down to three colors max.

EXERCISE

Look at your photos. Take out your notebook and write down elements of the room that need to be addressed that stand out to you at this point. Now write down you ideas about how to address these needs. You don't have to address everything at this point by the end of the book, you will have layers of ideas to get you started in designing your day.

CHECKPOINT

What you should have/know or considered at this point

- ✔ Main Wedding Colors,
- ✔ Complete favorites list,
- ✔ Possible number of guest,
- ✔ Where you wedding/reception will be held,
- ✔ Size of the space(s),
- ✔ Things you want to hide in the room,
- ✔ Things you want to emphasize in the room.

CHAPTER TWO

TABLE DESIGN

In considering your table setting, you will need to know the following: type of meal, is it a seated meal, buffet, cocktail party, lunch, etc. Once you know the type of meal you plan, you can being to design your table. For our purposes, we will focus on buffet dinner.

Step One:　How many food selections will you have? Will appetizers be served? Will alcohol be served? What types of alcohol? Drinks? Salad? Dessert(s)? Bread/butter?

These questions must be answered in order to know what pieces of china you will need. You can take your information to you rental store when you are ready to rent your china and it will make the process a lot easier.

Depending on the number of food selections, will determine the size of your dinner plate. You will need bowls if you serve salad. You will need separate plate for appetizers, bread and dessert. There are numerous pattern options for your china but you may be limited to choices depending on your rental store.

In addition to your china, you will need flatware for each plate/course. If you are unfamiliar with flatware, information is available online or your party rentals specialist can assist you.

What will you drink from? Now you will need to choose your stemware. If you are serving champagne, you will need a champagne glass. Wine drinkers will need a wine glass, brandy, whiskey, and so forth. Mixed drinks will also need to be considered. In addition to alcohol, I suggest having a water glass for guest who prefer water or a non alcoholic drink and/or coffee or tea cups if you decide on these beverage services.

Step Two: Now the hard part is out of the way, we can focus on the easy part. You need to pick your table linens. For basic options, you may want a floor length tablecloth or a table topper and skirt. From there, the options are limitless as far as patterned, textured, shiny, shimmery, overlays and cloths.

Don't forget napkins! Napkins also come in a number of patterns and designs. In choosing your napkin, you may want to consider if you napkins will be a part of the design or just utility. Napkins can be placed in several locations in your place setting, so where it is placed is as important as how it looks there.

NOTE: Make sure you are ordering the proper size linens for your tables.

Step Three: At this point, begin to think about how to accessorize your table. This is where you can refer back to your favorites list. Here you can consider incorporating some textures, shapes, animals, plants or other elements. We will touch on this further in the next chapter.

NOTE: We did not include food service in the text but it is something you will want to consider.

EXERCISE

Take out your notebook and write down what type of dinner and drink you want to consider. No final decisions have to be made at this point but having this information will help when you go to make you decision on dinnerware items. If there are certain pieces you know at this point you want to include, write it down. Do the same for linens and accessories.

CHECKPOINT

What you should have/know or considered at this point

- ✓ What food you will serve
- ✓ What drinks you will serve
- ✓ Dinnerware, Flatware and Stemware needs/options
- ✓ Table linen options
- ✓ Accessory possibilities/favorites

CHAPTER THREE

FLORAL DESIGN

Unless you are good with floral design and have a way to keep them fresh(if using fresh flowers), I would leave this area to the professionals. For best prices, consider in season florals and varying floral product in your color choice, unless you already know what you want. But, I will touch on a few points.

Option One: Try using free standing floral arrangements on pedestals around your room. It helps to fill the space, create drama, intimacy, and adds a layer of design to what was touched on in an earlier chapter.

Option Two: For table floral arrangements, think about the height of the room and your guests' views. You don't want arrangements that are too large or too small. An option is to have table arrangements of varying heights.

Option Three: Other places to use florals could be to hang them, use them at entrances, sprinkle petals, trees with lights and garland.

Refer back to your favorites list again for flower and plant favorites.

EXERCISE

Based on your vase choices from your favorites list, you now have shape choices of possible floral holders. Write in your design notebook your ideas on floral design and what you would like to have in the design.

CHECKPOINT

What you should have/know or considered at this point

- ✓ Whether or not to hire a professional
- ✓ Floral Options
- ✓ Where in your design floral choices will be used

CHAPTER FOUR

LIGHTING DESIGN

The last design element I would like to touch on is lighting. How will you use lighting in your room. Lighting plays a considerable role in pulling off the overall design of the room. Lighting helps to create the mood. You will need to decide what you want your light to do.

Options include: Candles, up-lights, spotlights, twinkle lights, chandeliers, luminaries, etc.

Be creative in how you use light but remember the key options: general, task, accent, and kinetic(moving).

General: Is needed to replace natural sunlight. Can be on a dimmer to reduce/increase the amount of light as needed.

Task: In certain areas, you will need task lighting. Photos, guest tables, food areas, musicians areas, etc. Light in these areas help to reduce accidents and risk. Only the minimum about of light necessary for each task is needed.

Accent: Is used to highlight elements of your design. Candlelight and up-lights would be considered accent lighting, as well as, luminaries and twinkles because they don't produce enough light to do a task or replace sunlight.

Moving: Is used mainly by musicians/djs. Strobe lights, flashers, chasers, etc. fit into this area.

CHECKPOINT

What you should have/know or considered at this point

- ✔ Type of lighting to use
- ✔ How choices will affect the design

CHAPTER FIVE

COMPLEMENTARY DESIGN
ELEMENTS

Menus and entertainment choices also play an important role in the overall effectiveness of your design. Make sure your selections complement the style of your wedding and accentuates the mood you are trying to create, instead of, being a distraction.

Now you have the basics to create a wedding that will incorporate your styles, personalities and truly reflect the wedding couple with a design that is all your own.